I0755921

FINISHING LINE PRESS
www.finishinglinepress.com

GOOD JOB

poems by

Jessica Farquhar

Finishing Line Press
Georgetown, Kentucky

GOOD JOB

ISBN 979-8-89990-388-5 First Edition

Publisher: Leah Huete de Maines
Editor: Christen Kincaid
Cover Art and Design: Sarah Flood-Baumann
Author Photo: Erin Chapman

Order online: www.finishinglinepress.com
also available on amazon.com

Author inquiries and mail orders:
Finishing Line Press
PO Box 1626
Georgetown, Kentucky 40324
USA

Contents

POET'S WORK 1

[When I cradle nightfall I become the new moon] 2

SEDUCTION OF MIMI 3

SYMPATHETIC MAGIC 4

LAST DAY 5

GOOD JOB AT STATE BAND 6

ARS POETICA 7

THE LAUNDRY DO-ER 8

NO RUSH 9

ODE TO TOTALITY 10

POETRY DESERT 11

A LITTLE OFF 12

DO YOUR BEST WORK 13

WAR PARTY 14

HERE IN THE LATE AFTERNOON OF OUR FANCY MEETING YOU LET IT ALL FADE OUT 15

HANDMAID TALES ARE PART OF THE MOST DANGEROUS GAME 16

HIGHER-UPS 17

TWENTY-FIVE-THOUSAND-DOLLAR PYRAMID 18

OMERTÀ 19

MIDLIFE MIDNIGHT 20

MATCH CUTS 21

ANATOMY OF A PALM TREE, OR, COASTAL PREMONITION BEFORE MY LAST DAY 22

GREAT REPLACEMENT 23

WEANING 24

SPECIAL WOUNDS 25

VOICE NAGGING SUSPICIONS 26

ARTIST STATEMENT 27
ANOTHER PREGNANCY DREAM 28
GRANDKIDS 29
ON THE OCCASION OF A BIRTHDAY 30
ON THE OCCASION OF A BIRTHDAY 31
A FEELING IN FEMALE FORM 32
LUXURY MEGA MERGER 33
MOON HOLDS MORE WATER IN MORE PLACES THAN EVER THOUGHT 34
AND AT TIMES THEY WILL SWARM YOU 35
PINBALL 36
ENDING YOUR FRIENDSHIP BRACELET 37
STAND DOWN 38
EEL'S NEST 39
OATMEAL BATH HOW-TO 40
GOOD MOOD 41
FIREWISE 42
WHAT BEGINNERS NEED TO KNOW 44
ALLOWANCE 45
BOSS FIGHT 46
SEVER 47
MONEY AND POWER 48
SONG OF EXPERIENCE 49
IN RAINBOWS 50
SOLAR POWER 51
APOPHENIC EPIPHANIES 52
NOTES + ACKNOWLEDGMENTS 53

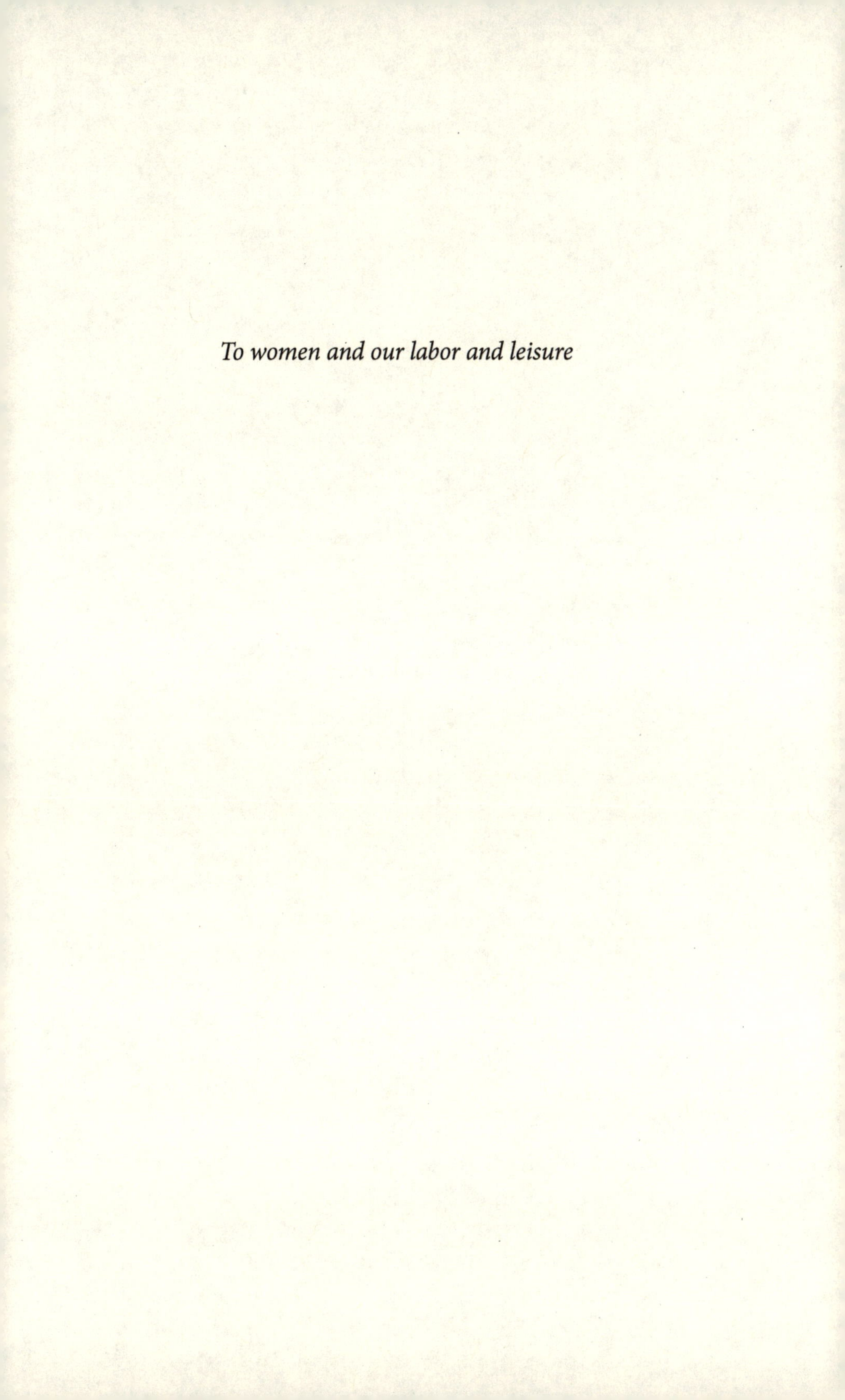

To women and our labor and leisure

POET'S WORK

after Lorine Niedecker

Grandmother
  advised me:
    Only say

the nice things.
  I sit at a desk
    by day, by night

write poems
  from this
    cemetery.

[When I cradle nightfall I become the new moon]

When I cradle nightfall I become the new moon
        and I make you crazy. I just want my one hit.

        Wonder what would happen if we up
and went to California? Would Nico puke every time

we got in the car and ruin a brand new t-shirt
        at Griffith Observatory. Or this time

        would we be able to make the whole trek
from national park to national park, no blooper reels,

just nailing every trick. When I make you crazy there
        are so many ways that can go: we fake our moon

        landing and just turn around and go home,
we spend all day poolside and watch the kids dive and dive,

we sneak outside the tent after everyone is asleep. I make
        the sky dark with my disappearing act.

SEDUCTION OF MIMI

When you tell me I am beautiful
you are saying my mother and father

made beautiful children. You are tiger drunk,
burning bright inside a cage again.

That same scared expression peers over a newspaper
as you whistle a national anthem. Why can't we

vote in secret and seduce in public, dive into
the sea with perfect hair and walk around

with shirts half-buttoned. I can take a compliment
and I can stop traffic, but I cannot keep my opinions

to myself. Typical. You don't see what's here.
You see what's not here.

SYMPATHETIC MAGIC

Piece of blood floating in the bathtub sanctuary, not a thread from the red towel rolled up or the red robe

Divider, provider

Endemic to this space program
turned trance frequency turned
commuter computer

is dwindling ovarian reserve

is such and such

caption captain

blue breath

inclined to edit less

LAST DAY

"I will live by my own policies." —Sinead O'Connor

I keep my binoculars ready, tiny
binoculars on a skinny string

given by my employer in thanks
for loyalty, in case the raptor

should return from the depths
of that treetop where she is home

-making. The bird is small
and I want to know her name. Yesterday

was Sinead O'Connor's last day
of her acquaintance with

this planet. I submit a sound
to the Merlin app, which says kite

is the bird's name. I hope to meet her
later in somebody's office.

GOOD JOB AT STATE BAND

The stadium smells of cream soda Dum-Dums
          only as bright as its brightest lights. Disappearing the band

          becomes audible. Legs march until they get there.
On the double in a world that lives in slow motion—

this is the discovery of extinction. Some kids are leaving earth,
          some are already grown up. They have known each other

          longer than they haven't,
a comfort in this town, a fur coat for adolescents

when they venture
          which is like never. I am sleepy, but I keep telling myself

          I have to wake up and make friends with these people.
Good Job is the name of this dream.

ARS POETICA

When I wake from my nighttime nap time
I notice the pattern in the foreign sheets:

Are they coral shells turned on their sides?
Are they leaves or little duck feet?

Some people like to say *pig gut*
and eat pea soup; some

charge low fees for wig cuts
out of their homes.

These people are my family
by relation and by choosing

hosting me, feeding me,
making their art and their living.

When I remove my eye mask
I don't always remove my mask mask.

THE LAUNDRY DO-ER

In the grand scheme of castellated landscapes what I need protecting from are mundanities so that when the preacher asks whose shirt shall I begin with I will hand yours over in a bundle because I am the laundry do-er. This morning's drive: deer grazing, dotted line, hawk over me, dotted line, there. Names are the only accuracies. In the cavities of our knowing we often pretend tied hands when so many trees need chopped and in truth we lumber in our sleep. Yes this, no that; is there really such a thing as overthink? In our miles-long survey of North Carolina hills, the equanimity of all is astounding. What the hills say, anyway.

NO RUSH

Way home from school drop-off guardians and parents drive as if to a dirge on the expressway. No rush just like those cops in Texas were in no rush.

No egret in the square window above my head. I imagine all the guardians and parents crying like I am crying out like the screaming in Texas when they learned it was their kids who weren't coming out.

Thurston tried to be a nature photographer this morning, but he said it was hard, the animals moved.

Last assignment of the year. Where is my egret? It was there yesterday and every day before that.

ODE TO TOTALITY

I lost my breath and found it
          in the C-shape of a transformed sun.

          All the slivers
projected on the ground through gaps

between children's fingers
          and leaf shadows—

          how we entertained ourselves
waiting for the big show,

the promised diamond fire:
          The sun's arms waved silver

          around the moon before its slender
body, reversed, shot out

from behind it. Ode to Stevie Nicks.
          Once it's over what's left is a bitten feeling.

POETRY DESERT

I said you might have just eaten my poem
to the child of my cousin who had remnants

of food in a bowl like shredded newspaper
in the dream. But I was half-teasing

and forgiving. Around me all the time now
I notice young men and wonder about

their lives, their living, and how they make it
because I have a son on the cusp of it,

manhood. Have they ingested enough poetry,
these young men, and will their *animas*

feed them the way I love to, standing
in the kitchen writing for hours on end.

Who will be the judge of that, but then
who will be the judge of *that*?

A LITTLE OFF

The cicadas are like *what the fuck.*
The geese's honks are a little bit off.

We think it's the weather. The squirrels
keep picking the habaneros off

and leaving them around the pot.
How do they *not* know? Off

with deadheads, daylilies pinched
at the ovary. Write it all off,

we are in our forties. At the intersection
of peak responsibility and off

the grid. Asking around but not
hearing most sounds. If we go off

the rails, we don't care. In fact,
we tell each other, *Hats off.*

DO YOUR BEST WORK

Homework's headline, but what does it mean
to do the work, my ex said in couples therapy

himself a budding therapist. Over a decade later
our son lacks task initiation,

afraid his best work won't be good. Reader,
this is my best work, pointing to the Milky Way

making sounds that mean I saw a shooting star
while asking for more dark, darker.

While floating in a spring-fed pool in the desert
thanking gods the only light is fire.

They didn't say it would be easy.
They said it would be worship. Or was it war

ship?

WAR PARTY

In this hide-out I hoard my white-out.
All the promises
here have heron shapes. We prepare
our war party
a ritual where we shed our mother shells
and be whatever
is under there; go to water
if scales
go to land if toenails. We are avoiding
the real issues
childbed fever, cadaverous particles
size 27.
It is safe here so I never go.
I just paint white
the inside of a tree trunk
with a tiny brush.

HERE IN THE LATE AFTERNOON OF OUR FANCY MEETING YOU LET IT ALL FADE OUT

The flora of fighters are lavender, aloe, and bombs that save. Wildlife of war: ravens and rats. You, soldier, smell like a snuffed out candle. Like ambivalence and everything's a threat. Whether you're here nor there. TBI or TMI. Crowns come together before you, never-father. Shiver feathers after the rub and turn, flailing with flails, mourning posts, stressing the strikes. You got out when you could. Forever aiming mortars.

HANDMAID TALES ARE PART OF THE MOST DANGEROUS GAME

In the stratosphere what do you choose to magnify, a heap of shit
talk or a dune of sand?

I found mounds of rage cloaked in the sounds
I manage to manage.

In your motion picture, what comes after the elk bugle
besides misty nostril spray?

More rage? A witch at the podium? Blurry deer? Heartbeat bills
are part of the endgame.

These days at seven o'clock it's dark. Which says something about
my mood

but nothing about the moon. I will wager that you underestimated
the pace at which

it dissolves, how many licks it takes for me to abandon this
altogether.

HIGHER-UPS

for Adam Lefton

They are not the Great Ones
because they are higher up.
There is law in the garden.
There is law in the garbage.
When you look up you point
to stars. When you look down
you hear your own anthem.
You tune in   to the distant
dog barks of your mind.
It is the law of creation.
What if we follow the sounds
of dogs barking? If we follow
that law we deal in magic.

TWENTY-FIVE-THOUSAND-DOLLAR PYRAMID

Untrammeled, unbloomed?
Unborn, too sober?
The pattern that cinnamon makes?
When you sprinkle it on bread?
A maze or cavern that goes on and on?
Cleaning up a mess with an ice cube?
Things you might wish for?
Taking risks in safe spaces?
Umbrellas in your tear ducts?
How much it costs to earn a lot?
Things you will never know?
Peppercorns, your partner's pelvis, molars?
Iliad battles and idiot ballads?
How some jellyfish are born?
The cloaks mollusks wear?
Opening and closing like an umbrella?
In order to move about?

OMERTÀ

code of silence meaning either humility or manliness

Imagine me as a ghost
(Freud is no longer a Freudian) But really what would you

say about me
if I weren't here. I am no longer here.

I am knolling my things in heaven
also known as the wood wide web, which has its secrets.

Heaven has its assassins, believe it or not. Imagine me
typing away, stacking paper, lining up pens and markers.

Tutored and tortured, imagine me
silent but moving so you can go ahead and say

whatever it is you are thinking about trees or fungus or
lunar learners such as myself.

There's still a next place to go on to
and a way to get there on this planet.

MIDLIFE MIDNIGHT

The damage I leave in my wake
          is my waking

          feverish sweat drop of a thought.

Imagine me as a boat, but
          I'm not so good

          on water.

At my wake, will you play
          My Life by Iris DeMent.

          I'll be busy

flying away on the back
          of a cicada.

          How long is the bridge

between this so-called pause
          and that final takeoff?

          Am I almost

out of my children

MATCH CUTS

Ten thousand times I have mothered, yet I am still
undiscovered. I can go places

that were mere field trips
to me once. I line up shapes of the past

with shapes of the future
making match cuts, shuffling cards, never surprised.

Alarmist search engine,
poetry is not a thing to be hacked. Army of bots

are my thoughts.
Sunflowers stalk them, teacher calls interrupt them like

the neighborhood cock
at five o'clock stirs us all.

ANATOMY OF A PALM TREE, OR, COASTAL PREMONITION BEFORE MY LAST DAY

I am pretty good at breathing.
          Gulls cast shadows across sand—
a buzz in the background

          cannot be made out.
In the dream he is at the podium.
          We shared air briefly.

Terminal inflorescence
          they named the flowers.
My toenails the color

          of a swimming pool floor.
The wind makes a thick sound
          in the fronds, pelicans

form themselves like a Thunderbird
          airshow, stiff wings &
quick turns; mourning

          doves make a song no one
cares about all fucking day.
          Old leaf is what they call

the dangling ones.
          In the dream at the podium
he says I am pretty good

          but he will be better.

GREAT REPLACEMENT

We can't be bothered with blinkers.
We are new SOBs with new cries.

Spring advice boils down to *Lemon* everything
Forge everything or *forge* everything.

Empty oceans make me more fearful
or less fearless:

an infinite sea of resolute tissue
aware of the actors acting, doing everything

in their power to escape the stinging pollinators.
This is the only explainer you are going to get

well-dweller in this flow of calamity.
Alternate nostril breathing is like this.

You're only as good as your last envelope
when the Great Replacement (true hoax)

sets in. The stars are falling, the stars are falling.
Insert tent pole metaphor.

I know someone who tried to die here.

WEANING

Like milking a cow,
hand-express what you're holding back,
in the shower. Warmth
and pressure will release
enough to shrink the breasts
(which swell after a day or so
of withholding) but not so much
your body will think
it's still nursing. Your heart might
want to keep nursing. Remember
the golden rule of breastfeeding,
The less you express, the less you make.
There will be engorgement,
inflammation;
it shouldn't be comfortable
thrusting your infant into boyhood.
For pain relief, make a bra salad:
Soften fresh green cabbage
leaves by rolling them
around in your hands. Place
torn pieces in your bra.
It's time to remove the cabbage
when it starts to smell cooked.
It's time to wean your son when
you've thought about it
long enough. No one tells you
how hard it's going to be, what takes
nursing's place. He likes best
nuzzling skull to skull,
one little arm around your neck.
He likes the new kind of love,
this eating cheerios in bed in the middle of the night.
Before the milk is gone, check
that your bond is set. Embed the child's heart
in your own wet cement heart. Then let
the drying commence.

SPECIAL WOUNDS

Wounds in wounds infrequently contained or flaming, bleeding *sometimes the hand is the physician waving its magic fix-it dust;* we are born with all of our eggs, wombs in wombs—when one opens the others spill out too. I wouldn't care if I were you. The dare inside the dare inside your wallet takes the shape of a fortune slip.

VOICE NAGGING SUSPICIONS

On the spectrum of spectrums I star
he stars they star we star. Forbid

myself from realizing
they duped me again, the administrators

the "counselors"
the psychologist who works for the school.

There are no allies here. Bulletin:
the Servant Superior is in. The menu

is full of reviews: salad review, soup
review, fruit review. The release police

had me sign some papers. The release police said
sigh it out. Sign here. Shy away.

Forgive me for not realizing.

ARTIST STATEMENT

I roam museums breathless
wishing I was brave

enough to bring a sketch-
book and a pouch of great

pencils. I know my mind better
than that. It thinks in shades

of words and roots and resents
artist statements. Stay in your lane

it wants to say to long paragraphs
written by sculptors who take

themselves seriously enough.
Museums are in trouble these days.

I must be given back, explains
the girl putting on her shoe.

ANOTHER PREGNANCY DREAM

I am past my prime. The pregnancy
is a realization I have looking down after

feeling womb movement. My mom occasionally
calls me princess even now that

I am forty-four. As a preschooler
I went to the library. I sounded out acrobat

on my own. Was Mom impressed?
My mom the diver who could back

dive, pike, and jackknife. My mom the swimmer
who could freestyle, butterfly, breaststroke.

I never was much of a swimmer.
Never learned the breaststroke.

Did she swim when she was my pool?
What on earth did she sound out?

GRANDKIDS

I'm worth whatever
they pay me.

We bleed yellow for our green
mothers who never learned shit.

Not every calculus
is calculation. Not every grade is bad or good.

At the end of the year
sometimes it's only

May or June, and across the landscape of generations it
means different things: birthday in a graveyard,

rejection by spawn,
corporate bonus structures, failing ninth grade.

Summer in springtime
is Mother Earth's way of catching up, having missed

the smell of hot dandelions
and her grandkids.

ON THE OCCASION OF A BIRTHDAY

The day I gave birth was not like any other day. It
was not like a day at all. It was more like a giant
diamond I was inside, famished. Looking out
through so many windows, I saw everything clear
and jumbled. So they brought me Lebanese food, the
oregano grit of za'atar bread well deserved. I
remember the bottle of champagne I picked up on
my way home, mid-contraction explaining to
the clerk I am going to have this baby in a few
hours. In the dim light of my bedroom, now, I
command them to pop it open, and each sip brings
new bubbles inside me. Yes, there is a baby; I
will get to that. Right now, I am piecing together
memories, prompting the midwife to tell me again
about shining her flashlight at me in the bathtub
every time I roared. No baby yet, no baby yet, no
bulging perineum even. The signs were there—me
gripping the entire lap of a woman sitting tub-side,
the doula, who urged hip rocking; long, loud grunts
that rose up from deeper than my cervix. I was
waiting for someone to announce his head. I
was leaning over the side of the tub. Usually, a
baby goes in and out, in and out. Mine was all the
way in, and then he was all the way out, in a *fell
swoop*, I was sure, and so I sat back in the
water. *That's it?* I said in a normal voice,
in a mom-for-the-second-time voice. No one
believed me. They had not announced a head.
The flashlight perked up, shone on a babe
stretched out under water. From water to water
spotlight on him. Next thing, he's on my chest
wrapped in a yellow towel, midwife scrubbing his back
hard to elicit that first, gentle, loud-as-he-can cry.

ON THE OCCASION OF A BIRTHDAY

Because the sky is lighting, I will deliver soon. For the first time,
coffee for midwife, husband, and mother, brewing since last night,
smells like a dark layer of air between me and them. This small tub
held me and water until it turned cold. *You should stay out of the
bath for a while*, my midwife says to my body. I drape with robe
over a giant blue ball and reach out for two hands, lean back into
someone else's hands. Am I thirsty? I should drink water.
By the look of the pink-gray sky, I have been laboring a whole
night. There is a birthing soundtrack, but I hear mostly my mother
deeply Ohm-ing. I see Christmas lights strung around windows,
midwife taking notes or smiling from her station in the corner.
I smile when she asks if she can go fill her daughter's stocking.
What I feel is relief—compress warm on low belly; finally, then
crashing down life: release. Squiggly light captured on film.

A FEELING IN FEMALE FORM

You can see the sea out there
if you can see it. You sit

on a paper moon on the edge
of an anniversary party

with paper flowers in your hair.
Swing your legs, pucker your lips.

Go ahead and blow a kiss to the stars.
How to be someone named Billy:

play the piano, practice your accent.
Be prepared. When the party

goes from June to July
don't wait for the fireworks

to tell you it's time to go home.

LUXURY MEGA MERGER

Rhymes with murder. Only mergers
in the building. I thought Tapestry

was a Carole King album but now I hear
it is a house of luxury, in quotes.

Apparently luxury has been facing a downturn.
Rhymes with brown fern. Which reminds me.

My Queen Kimberlys are thirsty and want
their fronds doused. My routine is all

messed up because they cancelled school
again, this time because of the bus issues.

Driver shortage, too many stops, staggering
start times still might be a good idea.

I thought *luxury* had no roots, would you believe
it comes from *brightness*. No comment.

MOON HOLDS MORE WATER IN MORE PLACES THAN EVER THOUGHT

I drew you a map of my life. When you died it was found
in your pocket. I make the most sound

decisions, the ones you call messes. My thoughts blister over once
you're done hearing them.

My permanent half-mast heart. Lost. They see me and I look
lost because I'm lost.

Pouring water in craters, dipping water from around me
like a child in a bathtub.

Mistaken for the widow again.

AND AT TIMES THEY WILL SWARM YOU

Dude was doomed. Outside this city
was a tight turn he took drunk

listening to what? We'd all like
to know.

Started out as a fish. How did it
end up like this? Like a thing

you could swallow. Like a pair
of golden handcuffs or sunglasses

that perch atop your head when
all you can think about

is how to put things more
delicately.

A woodpecker drills somewhere.
The mid-yard fire pit is a boardroom for birds.

The perfectionists give you nothing
but permission to flee. What the fuck

are the neighbors laughing at.

PINBALL

Shiny moon against dark blue
    is a pinball

    machine quarter
halfway in the slot. *Ding-ding-ding*

is the sound dreams make
    banging their heads

    against a bell. Some say
self-help vigilance guarantees against aging

disgracefully, but there is evidence
    to the contrary.

    Flat pillows after all
make flat dreams. White noise drowns

out children but not parents, whose voices
    are trapped

    inside you.
The sounds coming out of my mouth

originated in the belly of my mother.
    We release

    them like a
shot that's been slung, like a shiny ball.

ENDING YOUR FRIENDSHIP BRACELET

You and I are born from folding, according to the origami
artist. According to the daydream scientist

we are born from a watercolor gaze. This is unconventional,
I know, spending a Friday afternoon with sun in our eyes

weaving together orange, pink, and marigold threads so we
can say in a new way *I love you.*

I fucked up that one part so you would know that I am not God. At
the air archive, I took a sample from each tank and

felt more limber. As instructed, I tie a knot to end the
bracelet. If I love you I will search for your poems in all the

bookstores New York City has.
I will photograph the spines so you can see your name.

STAND DOWN

Some account services require you to stand off
or at least

stand down until further notice   Do you need a password
reset

We are on high alert until further notice Can you dial in
to the afternoon

powwow after you rotate back into the lineup or
do lunch

tomorrow afternoon We need to transform our language
and bring

our binoculars from now on so we know if that is a falcon
on its way

back or just some hawk we are thinking about hiring
when it lands

EEL'S NEST

In the close reading of my bathtub
I am a fish wife
yelling the names of fish I have to sell at market
and stinking
I come down from my eel's nest when I hear
the song of
the bowhead whale I sing
as I clean
I yell as I sell *One man's vulgarity*
is another
man's lyric I experiment with feelings
and with this
I fantasize my way through chores
my arms
my lungs are sore

OATMEAL BATH HOW-TO

1\.
Why not learn something today, something about milking oats in a cheesecloth bundle, taking that kind of a tepid bath.

2\.
Maybe it's noon or maybe it's something else. But the bells the bells the bells. Something about the number twelve.

3\.
For my next trick I'll calm myself down. Next to the children I feel as big as a whale's heart and as hot.

4\.
There was a pattern to that brick patio. It went in rectangular circles. It went somewhere poisonous, and lonely.

5\.
I'm damned if I do, and I always do. Dear motorcycle enthusiast. Troubleshooting. Empty tank. Put fuel in tank.

6\.
My first-ever bout of poison ivy or -oak started there; the grab,
the rush, the oil molecule.

7\.
What if the whole world wasn't out to get me. Not the mother otters holding their babies amidst the seaweed. Neither the river otters.

GOOD MOOD

Congratulations I tell myself
you are forty and you are finally
done pouting

My birthday gift to you
is to look more
into mirrors

I went to sleep with
a bang and woke up with *a cough*

transformed overnight
into a down vest-
wearing woman

What can I say
the temperature dropped
Ok Charlie!

is my favorite command
I learned from the Kennel Club
It is the release

after a lot of hard work
paying attention and
taking orders because

you want to have a job any job
When I lose my voice
it always comes back better

FIREWISE

1.
Cactuses and clouds pile here like each other
(like they like each other)

in this illustrated guide to disappointment.
None the wiser to what might really happen

ever I dream my toes are cut off and stitched back on
and even though it seems like they're on wrong,

I have to trust that their new nature is ok.
It seems like this is the only body I've ever had

but I know there was one before and one before that.
I play it off and walk awkward.

The gila woodpecker flies from one saguaro
to another saguaro; the scratchy sound is the wind

rubbing itself against the tall ones. The desert palette
is nothing to complain about.

2.
When I no longer have words to describe fire
I know the wind

is in control. Slipstream city. Craggy warmth,
lawful war.

It is clear whom I must protect and whom
I can shoot.

Master of surrender, master of slippery
coping—

I offer my rolled ankle at a temple
where heads rolling

was once a game. Now anything less than murder
is love.

I adapt and grab the rope. I climb up the stairs
to a point.

WHAT BEGINNERS NEED TO KNOW

Do not buy tandem fishing kayaks unless
you are at least fifty years old and own a vest you would like

to spangle to show your fashion sense.
If you are into camping, you can wait for the catalog

to come out to get the specs. The sharp red stern of your water toy points to the horizon

and where we will have a picnic lunch on the sand.
There you can unclasp your life jacket and remove

it if you wish. We don't have the breakdown yet.
Literally, you were in Seattle yesterday drinking limeade

and walking among the junipers. Everything you want
to do is a breeze. Take it from me. Can you say f-u-c-k?

Of course you can. Of course you can. Take it from me.

ALLOWANCE

If there is a time
I'm supposed to
show up, no one
ever told me it.
Sometimes we make
love in the morning.
Then I need a smoothie
on my way in-
to the office. Sometimes
on Fridays there is
a deposit. The church bell
tolls is how I know
what time it is. I'd rather
ask for nothing than
permission. I am a doctor
of something, and everyone
should call me that.
Specializing in bathing
my own feet at the end
of a "long" "day."
At the end of the world
with salt and peppermint;
floating flower petals
my eyes covered by
a hand-sewn sack filled
with the seed of persimmon.

BOSS FIGHT

You can gauge the time by the
blue of the broken, bangin' ocean's
blasted veneer. My youngest
tries to defuse monsters,
but weasels preen, and monkeys are
bossy. They fidget and they're ready
to fight. They fume, forage for
trouble, bleed for glamour.
The song says they fuck up the shots.

SEVER

I did indeed procure the severance through a parlay
of risky negotiations. The only spice derived

from conifers, I present you the juniper berry,
an aromatic experience best lived firsthand

so don't take my word for it. Separate
the seed cone to get the spice and make the gin

in order to prepare for the day the separation
becomes official, golden parachute in hand.

No more vipers in sight, no more repertories
on the schedule. Just me and the parent

of the calf I heard as it entered the world
last night. A message only the Fates could bring:

Mothers, as we enter the impasse known as Postpartum
we must leave our parasols behind.

MONEY AND POWER

Good morning, good money. Siri
doesn't know the difference. Like how

my dog noses the cicada shell as if
it might come alive. We have good mornings.

We make good money. We wish good mornings
to others and good money too.

Tacky to say it, I know. But just listen
to that Liz Phair song about shitloads

of money, and you will know what I mean.
Mornings are better when there's money

in the bank, more money on the way,
and even some you can give away.

When I was little I wanted to be the cashier
with all her power, pressing the register keys.

SONG OF EXPERIENCE

What do you want me
to have done? I have
done it. Sung it, swung it, spun it.

You. Wizard. Will come to
a dark wood and follow
the sound of hounds barking
at invisible foxes.

Who tosses whom and
to what beast? This is
your feast, your lore
no longer, my lord.

Grant me a shanty,
a home, you gnome.
I have bled the dead,
freed the steed, done

the tasks you asked, my
liege, my deed.

IN RAINBOWS

Let the shame be his
or hers or anyone else's

because my spiritual acumen is lit.
My shadow follows

me around like a dog
and I tell it to lay down.

You, hater, are shit
and you can't have this

or this. Gradient
of rhyme

this rainbow shines in
mountain time

super arch over closed-down
mines. Calm city on wheels.

SOLAR POWER

Flower power, what is that? Spending hours outdoors
in excessive heat experts warned about,

now that is a certain kind of power. In the pool,
the bugs float by, some looking like feathers.

Once again hot from the inside, pick your poison.
Not a fever, scientifically speaking. Clouds are weak,

floating like dead bugs, shielding sunbathers zero.
It's the temperature, the humidity, the lack

of water inside the body causing nausea
after hours of it. Not to mention mezcal.

Tight clothing, too much movement, all whose fault.
Ignoring red exclamation marks, the health department calls

and all things apocalyptic, although if honesty
is a thing, all things have become apocalyptic.

APOPHENIC EPIPHANIES

We abandoned the abandoned quarry
The end of the world is taking so long

We are ready for hand-holding culture; nations built by Kali; few
green shoots lit up by polluted skies

I tossed small crocs up the beach before the tide could eat
them

I've had kids; I know how time moves for mothers, like a wave
forming then crashing

Vacation is migration from one state to another, dance-off
with weather

Little skulls pinned to our vests
Lifting our babies up to the skies

NOTES + ACKNOWLEDGMENTS

In the mode of a cento/telestich/golden shovel poem, the last words of each line in "Boss Fight" combine to read "The Ocean's Youngest Monsters Are Ready for Glamour Shots," the title of a *New York Times* article by Erik Olsen.

"Seduction of Mimi" was inspired by Lina Wertmüller's *Seduction of Mimi* on the occasion of her death.

Poems in this book have appeared in: *ABZ, Autocorrect, Cream City Review, Entrance Journal, The Journal, Transom*, and *Western Humanities Review.* Grateful acknowledgment is extended to Magnificent Field Press for publishing the chapbook *Dear Motorcycle Enthusiast*, where some of these poems also appeared.

Love + Gratitude

Eternal thanks to the teachers who made me: Maureen Morehead, Jeffrey Skinner, Paul Griner, Sena Jeter Naslund, Marianne Boruch, Don Platt, and the GOAT Mary Leader.

MFA friends who read my work with so much care: Corey Van Landingham, Jacob Sunderlin, Joshua Diamond.

Sublimity City siblings forever: V. Joshua Adams, Emma Aprile, Ann DeVilbiss, Kristina Erny, Danielle Fleming, Hailey Higdon, Parker Hobson, John James, Kristi Maxwell, Kristen Miller, Ken Walker, and Kate Welsh.

Thank you to the Kentucky Foundation for Women for decades of support for my activist and artmaking work. To the Sisters of Loretto Motherhouse for hosting me in the little house among the cows, for the meals, and for the work you do.

Amanda Thompson, thanks for the flowers.

My birth attendants, Juliet, Susan, and Aundria, and all the midwives and doulas.

Dr. C., thank you for teaching me to take my dreams seriously.

OSM JOBS—my work sisters Olivia DeJesus, Brittni Caudill, Sara Nelson.

The families of origin—Farquhars and Fanellis, all. But especially my mama, Linda Fanelli.

Deep eternal love and gratitude to my kids, who also made me: Thurston & Nico.

And I can never thank enough the ultimate partner in all things, Mark Campbell.

Jessica Farquhar's previous collection is the chapbook *Dear Motorcycle Enthusiast* (The Magnificent Field Press). Her recent work appears in *Autocorrect, Entrance Review, Red Branch Review, Sarabande's Once a City Said: A Louisville Poets Anthology,* and *You Blew It: A Miracle Monocle Micro-anthology.* She is the recipient of multiple grants from the Kentucky Foundation for Women and was selected as a KFW Artist in Residence at Loretto Motherhouse. Jessica holds an MFA from Purdue University, where she served as the assistant director of Creative Writing. After eleven years of working in corporate strategy and leadership development at a Fortune 50 healthcare company, she is now an independent consultant. A founding member of the Sublimity City poetry collective based in Louisville, Kentucky, she has taught creative writing workshops throughout the Louisville Free Public Library system and has given readings in the region. You can follow her adventures in motorcycle riding and poetry writing on Substack.

www.ingramcontent.com/pod-product-compliance
Lightning Source LLC
LaVergne TN
LVHW090537110826
845146LV00003B/1142
9798899903885